The Adventures of Scuba Jack
Copyright 2022 by Beth Costanzo
All rights reserved

Mr. Sprinkles and I were the best of friends.

On a brisk day in October, we had a ceremony for Mr. Sprinkles. Mom said a prayer and then Dad, Mom, and I shared our favorite Mr. Sprinkles story. The following day, we made a scrapbook for Mr. Sprinkles and put all our favorite pictures in it.

Talking about Mr. Sprinkles made me feel better.

Each day Mr. Sprinkles, and I played hide and seek. Mr. Sprinkles hid, and I found him.

We played fetch, too! Mr. Sprinkles didn't bring the stick back to me. I don't think he understood the game.

Mr. Sprinkles loved to play dress up.

Birthday parties were his favorite event. He licked all the excess frosting from my face! YUK!

Mr. Sprinkles didn't love to brush his teeth. The toothpaste was too minty!

When I felt sick, Mr. Sprinkles always made me feel better.

We loved camping together. Mr. Sprinkles hogged all the blankets!

One day I came home from school and Mr. Sprinkles didn't run to me. Mom said he wasn't feeling well and she would take him to the vet. A vet is a doctor who takes care of animals.

The next day when I got home from school, Mr. Sprinkles wasn't in his bed. "Mom, where is Mr. Sprinkles?" I asked. Mom looked very sad, and her eyes were puffy like she had been crying. Mom said, "Come, sit next to me." "Okay," I said. "I took Mr. Sprinkles to the vet. While the vet examined Mr. Sprinkles, he passed away." "He passed away. What does that mean?" I asked. "It means he went to heaven. He won't be coming home."

I hugged Mom tightly and started crying. Mom cried too! Mom said, "It's okay to feel sad when you lose a loved one. It's okay to talk about your feelings, and cry. Each time we cry, we release our emotions. This helps our bodies towards healing from the loss of Mr. Sprinkles. Mom and I always talked about Mr. Sprinkles with love.

Mom said the pain of losing Mr. Sprinkles will go away, but the wonderful memories will always remain. I think Mom is right! I loved Mr. Sprinkles and he loved me! Some people will never understand how much I loved my dog, but that's okay, Mr. Sprinkles did. He was my favorite "hello" every day and my hardest "goodbye!" I love you Mr. Sprinkles.

My pet was a ☐

My pet's name was ☐

The things I loved most about my pet are

_____
_____
_____
_____

The things I miss most about my pet are

_____
_____
_____
_____

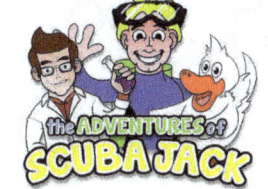

Forever with Me!

I will never forget

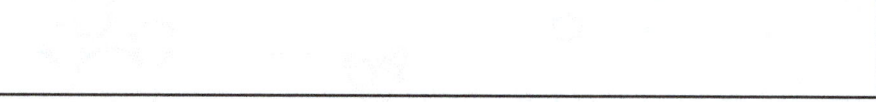

Place a photo of your pet here

My Pet

My pet's name:

What Animal's kind was my Pet?

How old was my Pet when I got it?

Who chose its name?

What was my Pet's favorite food?

What did my Pet like to do?

My Pet was special because:

www.ingramcontent.com/pod-product-compliance
Lightning Source LLC
Chambersburg PA
CBHW060428010526
44118CB00017B/2414